GOD'S GOT A BETTER IDEA

God's Got a Better Idea

Billy Zeoli

Fleming H. Revell Company
Old Tappan, New Jersey

Scripture references identified KJV are from the King James Version of the Bible.

Scripture references identified LB are from The Living Bible, Copyright © 1971 by Tyndale House Publishers, Wheaton, Illinois 60187. All rights reserved.

Library of Congress Cataloging in Publication Data

Zeoli, Billy.
    God's got a better idea.

    Includes index.
    1. Prayers. 2. Ford, Gerald R., 1913– —Religion. I. Title.
BV245.Z46   242'.8   78-64373
ISBN 0-8007-0933-0

For Jerry and Betty,
two of God's better ideas—
remembering, as I always do,
your love, your concern, your sharing
of everything you are and have

AN APPRECIATION
by
Gerald R. Ford

When I was asked to write this Appreciation for *God's Got a Better Idea*, I was honored, but, I must admit, I was somewhat uncertain about which course to follow. Should my words be directed toward the material which in itself is irrefutable since it is based upon the Bible? Or should they be focused on the man who prepared it, Billy Zeoli, an irrepressible Christian, a religious leader of tremendous influence? Either presented a substantial challenge. Ultimately I chose the man because I have come to recognize him as an alter ego, a second self. Let me explain.

Admittedly, Billy and I are each blessed with a wonderful wife and family.

For many years we have called Michigan our home state.

Also, we have a mutual interest in sports, particularly football—Billy through his own special and widely acclaimed ministry among its professional athletes, and myself as a former player who remains an avid fan.

And I suppose you could say that our chosen careers have kept us both in the public arena—his as the man and mentor behind Gospel Films, Inc., which is involved in the production of evangelistic motion pictures spreading the Word of God worldwide, and mine in law, and in the

7

legislative and executive branches of our government.

But perhaps the greatest bond which exists between us is that we have both put our trust in Christ, our Saviour, and have relied on Him for direction and guidance throughout our lives.

Lastly, we share a friendship which has transcended the years, with love and respect and understanding.

It is that *understanding* which I wish to consider here in these few pages—Billy's singular brand. The capacity to be thoroughly familiar with the character and propensities and problems of one's fellowman is a rare quality, indeed. Billy Zeoli possesses that golden gift and shares it with many. He shared it with me, and *God's Got a Better Idea* corroborates that.

In the fall of 1973, shortly after my nomination to fill the vacancy in the office of Vice-President of the United States, there began arriving every Monday morning at my desk a message from Billy. Each contained a Verse from Scripture and a Prayer relating to that Verse which he had especially written for me. He sent them under the heading of "God's Got a Better Idea."

Those weekly messages followed me into the Oval Office and continued throughout my presidential tenure. There were 146 in all. Not only were they profound in their meaning and judicious in their selection, I believe they were also divinely inspired. Billy Zeoli was the instrument.

Historians may one day draw a correlation between the events of those three years and the contents of the pages, so thoughtfully composed and here—in this volume—reproduced. I leave that to them.

I can only say that I was deeply affected by each of the "Ideas." Some served as inspiration, some as guidance, some to assuage the fear and foreboding in the making of important decisions, and some to carry me through times of personal crises.

Billy touched upon many areas—love, responsibility, criticism, attitude, sensitivity, trust, values, wisdom, worship, even Christmas, and always with that inherent sense of *understanding*.

Two in particular come immediately to mind. One relates to righteousness, the other to my "five treasures," my wife and four children.

In the former he chose this Verse: "Righteousness exalteth a nation; but sin is a reproach to any people" (Proverbs 14:34 KJV). His accompanying Prayer is moving in its simplicity: "I thank You for the privilege I have not only as a citizen of 'God's Country,' but as a citizen of the United States of America. I am grateful for the pride I feel when I think of what this Nation has accomplished. Father, do not let this great Country drift further from the true spiritual moorings which made us what we are. May I, as a person, and this Nation as a whole, be guided by moral and spiritual objectives. May our righteousness exalt this Nation. Guide us so that we do not follow the path of expediency and find reproach upon us."

While this "Idea" reflected upon my public life, the following one touched upon my private life and intuitively Billy knew of my need to be sensitive to and grateful for its gifts: "The Lord hath done great things for us; whereof we are glad!" (Psalms 126:3 KJV). It elicited this meditation: "Lord, help me never, even unconsciously, to hide my love for my wonderful wife and four precious children. They stand in the reflected glare of my public office and just by being my family endure pressures not experienced by other Americans. Keep me mindful of their needs, with time to listen to their problems and sensitivity to be understanding, even when they don't bother to confide. Thank you for these five treasures!"

Understanding, Billy's unique gift, manifested itself early in childhood. I have heard him tell the story of his father, a burglar and a drug addict, a penniless Italian who never got beyond the fifth grade. The Philadelphia ghetto was his home and his teachers, street hoodlums.

For his crimes he was sent to prison. One day a copy of the New Testament was tossed into his cell. Upon opening it his eyes rested on the passage, "Heaven and earth shall pass away, but my words shall not pass away" (Matthew 24:35 KJV), and it changed his life. When he was released from prison, he became an ordained Baptist minister and would captivate his congregation with stories of his past and how the Lord had changed him.

In the words of the son, "He married my mother, who was singing in the church choir while studying for the opera. I was born in Philadelphia and as a youngster had to stay in the church basement during my father's confessions. My parents did not want me to know about his past sins. But when I was six, I happened to reach up and turn the dials of the loudspeaker system that carried his voice downstairs. I heard it all, and had more love and understanding of my father than ever before. I decided then to follow him in the ministry."

Although the Verses and Prayers in *God's Got a Better Idea* were initially directed to me, they are for all believers in His Word, for all who would seek His help. It is an honor and a privilege to share them. I am eternally indebted to Billy Zeoli for *his* understanding.

PREFACE

"What is he like?" people ask me. "What is Gerald Ford *really* like?"

Curiosity about a man who was President of the United States is natural, and people want to know about Gerald Ford. What kind of man is he close up, away from the television cameras, newspaper photos, and the imposing trappings of the White House? Apart from the press conferences, the formal speeches, and the glitter of the most powerful office in the world, what kind of person is he, really?

People ask *me* about Gerald Ford because we are friends, and our friendship has been widely publicized. In a way, it's something any person with a normal-sized ego must get used to, being known as "a friend of ————," especially if the "friend" is President of the United States. You pick up a newspaper or magazine and see yourself described as "a friend of ————," and, at first, it does require a certain ego adjustment! But this friendship is so rich, so important, it is worth that and much, much more. The kind of friendship I have with Gerald Ford can happen only when one's friend is an extraordinary individual—like Gerald Ford.

So, whenever people ask me about him, want to know what kind of person he *really* is, I enjoy talking about him. He is one of the most remarkable men I've ever met.

What is so extraordinary about Jerry Ford? What are the

11

characteristics that set him apart from ordinary men? First of all, I think, his integrity . . . his rocklike loyalty . . . his fairness toward people and genuine concern for them . . . his total lack of pretension . . . his ability to laugh at himself and acknowledge his mistakes. And always— perhaps most of all—his willingness to rely on God, to let his faith in Christ operate quietly, constantly, in his everyday life. Those things and more I could tell you about Gerald Ford. Perhaps they sound like the standard list of admirable qualities, but I have seen them lived out in Ford's life so many times that I will rarely use the words *honest, loyal, compassionate,* again, without thinking of him.

If you could see him in all the circumstances and situations that I have seen, you would know exactly what I mean.

I first met my congressman, Jerry Ford, in 1963 when I called on him in his congressional office in Grand Rapids, Michigan. While I was sitting in his outer office, a couple came out of his private office; a very heavyset woman—I mean *heavyset*—and her very skinny husband. She was poking him in the ribs and saying, "I told you! If you had come to see Jerry about this a week ago, he'd have taken care of it *then*."

I started to laugh. Just then Congressman Ford appeared in the doorway, saw me laughing, and smiled. The rapport between us was immediate.

During the next eight or nine years, we were together fairly regularly. In Washington, it was for events such as the prayer luncheons for athletes which were held in the congressional dining room. Mr. Ford and I served as cochairmen. Jerry enjoys being with professional athletes. When he was in Grand Rapids, we would meet for discussion and prayer together.

Neither Jerry nor I suspected it, but God was drawing us together for a special friendship.

In late summer of 1973, Congressman Ford asked me to bring my wife, Marilyn, and our children to Washington that fall to open a session of the House of Representatives with prayer. We went down in October, and, after checking into a hotel, we found a sidewalk cafe and sat down to eat. A young man came running along the sidewalk shouting and cheering.

"Hey," I asked, "what's going on?"

"Don't you know? Vice-President Agnew just resigned!"

I had prepared a prayer to read before the House of Representatives the next morning. I was convinced it was at least as good as Martin Luther's Ninety-five Theses. When I read it to Marilyn, she said, "Z, it isn't you. It doesn't sound like you, and you don't read it well." She was right. This, with the important new development of the Agnew resignation, caused me to return to the hotel to prepare another prayer.

The next morning, Marilyn and I took the children to Jerry's office in the House of Representatives' wing of the Capitol Building. He was then minority leader of the House, and his name was being suggested all over Washington that day as a possible nominee for the Vice-Presidency. After I had delivered the prayer, my family and I stayed on to observe the proceedings for about an hour, and then Jerry took us downstairs to the House dining room. Film crews from the major networks were after him for his comments on the vice-presidential situation. Congressional leaders of both parties were saying, "This is the man for the job!" They obviously regarded him as a man of integrity and impeccable character. I placed a note on his office desk as my family and I left the House of Representatives. The note said that I believed he was the man whom God had chosen for that job. It was not really my style to do that sort of thing. It was part of the special relationship which I believe God was creating between Jerry and me.

Two days later, we saw the television announcement of Gerald R. Ford's nomination to the office of Vice-President of the United States.

Shortly after that Washington visit, I mentioned to Jerry my idea of sending him a memo every week. He was enthusiastic. We decided to call it "God's Got a Better Idea." I arranged to mail one each Friday from my Gospel Films office in Muskegon, Michigan, timed to reach him the following Monday. The first one was dated October 22, 1973. Here on the following page is the format I used while Mr. Ford was Vice-President and later President.

Jerry always managed to let me know that he appreciated the weekly "Idea"; sometimes it was a personal call or letter, sometimes it was through a staff member. Subsequently, I visited Jerry in Washington almost every month. We spent time talking and reading the Word of God, and praying together.

I spent the summer of 1974 in Switzerland to study at L'Abri with Dr. Francis A. Schaeffer and had prepared twelve "God's Got a Better Idea" devotionals before leaving, so that one could be sent to Jerry each week as scheduled. The news from home was full of Watergate and there were indications that President Nixon could not survive politically. Early in August, the European press was predicting that Nixon's presidency would end soon, either through resignation or by impeachment. I telephoned

GOD'S GOT A BETTER IDEA

Week of October 22, 1973

To Jerry
From Billy

VERSE
Deuteronomy 10:12
King James

#1   "What doth the Lord thy God require of Thee

            but to fear the Lord thy God

            to walk in all His ways,

            and to love Him,

            and to serve the Lord thy God

            with all thy heart and with all thy soul."

PRAYER

My Dear Lord,

May I learn to fear Thee because I want to, not because I have to.

May I learn to walk in your ways because they lead up right paths.

May I love You not just because You first loved me, but because I
            want to give You my love.

May I serve You not to be in Your good graces, but to find the inner
            peace of serving God.

May my doing this with all my heart and soul not only be known to You
            but may it be apparent to my fellowman so that
they may honor You by saying,

            "This man has been with Jesus!"

                              In the Name of the Risen Son Jesus,

                                        Amen

Jerry at his home in Alexandria, Virginia. His spirit was warm, and he would not predict what was going to happen. I suggested that we pray together when I returned to the States.

Jerry said, "You can pray there now, and I can pray here now."

Linked together from Bavaria to Virginia by much more than a telephone cable, we prayed audibly for God's wisdom and guidance.

Does it matter that the President of the United States has a deep personal faith in God? Does it really make any difference to have a Christian in the White House? I believe it does. Jerry Ford understood the principles and values of the Word of God, and consequently he had a perspective, a philosophy, a frame of reference that is different. Throughout his presidency he would wrestle constantly with the questions: "What are the moral implications here? What is the *right* thing?" His Christian philosophy of life would give him constant concern that he not do merely the easy thing, or the politically expedient thing, but the *right* thing in the moral sense. Yes, it makes a great deal of difference to have that kind of man in the White House.

On August 9, 1974, Gerald Ford's inaugural speech reached us through a portable radio in Germany. It was a very emotional moment for us. I know that the words he shared from his heart that day moved this nation to new hope and courage. It was one of those moments when the bonds that hold people together in Christ were particularly strong.

I had promised to call Jerry when we returned home. It was a new experience to call the White House, and I left word that I had phoned, not really expecting a reply that day. The call came less than an hour later. I was surprised to hear Jerry's voice. I didn't know whether to call him Mr. President, Jerry, or Mr. Ford. I ended up putting them all together and it came out poorly. He suggested that I call him Jerry—just as I always had—and I did. He talked with everyone in my family and wanted to make sure that I was coming to Washington in three days for our usual Bible study and prayer. Frankly, because of his new responsibilities I really thought that our meeting might have to be postponed.

"Are you able to come, Billy?"

"I certainly am."

"Are you too busy to make it?"

"No, I'll make it."

"Well, come on, and I'll see you at one-thirty."

"Jerry, I'm a little confused. I don't know how to get into the White House. What do I do?"

"Just tell them you're coming to see me, and use my name. It will really work wonders."

I did just that, and it did work wonders!

I'm a very patriotic person and admittedly emotional at times. My first visit to the Oval Office was such an occasion. I walked in, put my arm around the President of the United States. We chatted for a while, then read from the Bible, and prayed together.

That was the beginning of three exciting years of sharing the positive message of Christ with President Ford, through both good and difficult situations. We met every four or five weeks and eventually moved our time alone together from the Oval Office to the upstairs family quarters in the White House. Our monthly prayer time would begin with breakfast—just the two of us—in the private dining room. We would read the Word of God and pray together. Then I would walk with him to the Oval Office, visit with a few friends, before going to spend time with the First Lady, Mrs. Betty Ford. It was never routine. Sharing with people whom you love that much, at a place like the White House, could never become commonplace!

I saw Gerald Ford as President in good times and bad, and I got to know something about the man. I saw his warmth toward others, his concern in little things—there was the time he offered to have my son Steve come to the White House so he could encourage him about his grades at school: "Let me talk to him, Billy. I've had three boys. You just stay out of it and let me talk to him." I felt his concern when Marilyn broke her leg skiing and was hospitalized. The Fords called three times in one day to check on her and to offer suggestions about my running the household in her absence!

When I say that Jerry is unpretentious, I remember little things: the time when my visit to the White House was longer than usual, he picked up the phone and asked one of his staff to cancel a plane reservation for me. He then arranged for me to spend the night at the White House. Or the way he would apologize for security precautions around him—even after two assassination attempts. Sometimes he would hear jokes told about himself on television and laugh at those that poked fun at him. He never came to think of himself as bigger-than-life, nor was he hypersensitive to criticism, even when he thought it was unfair. He listened, squared his shoulders, and went on. He's that kind of man.

When I talk about his integrity and his courage, I'm not just using empty words. Time after time I saw him in the pressures of the world's toughest job. He would not budge an inch from his basic principles. For all his warmth and gentleness, he is a tough, resilient man. Nothing ever bent him away from his bedrock values. He is made of sturdy stuff, Gerald Ford, and when he found himself, unexpectedly, in the toughest job on earth, facing the task of pulling together a divided, disillusioned nation, he measured up. He was strong enough to get the job done.

Jerry Ford has vast inner resources, and his faith in God is an important part of that. He is a growing, maturing disciple of the Lord Jesus Christ, a thinking Christian. Christianity for him is an internal personal matter, never something to call attention to. He could have done many things to get political mileage from his Christian life, but he stoutly refused to do so. Faith in God, to the Fords, is a personal and a family matter, a source of strength. One gets the feeling that, whatever they face, they'll come through because they trust in God and in each other.

In September of 1974, I was on a preaching mission in Findlay, Ohio. I had finished the evening service and gone to dinner when I received an urgent phone call from my wife. Betty Ford was to undergo a biopsy and possibly further surgery the next morning. I made a phone call to Washington and reached another friend of the Fords, who told me, "Betty wants you to come to see her before she goes into the operating room."

Arranging for a flight out of Findlay, Ohio, in the early hours of the morning wasn't easy.

I arrived at the hospital an hour before the operation was to begin. I spent a few minutes with Betty, reading the Bible and praying. She was such a confident person—so certain that this was what must be done, whatever the findings would be. Admiral Lukash, the Fords' White House doctor, was there with us some of the

time. Susan Ford arrived later. What the doctors had suspected was true, and it was necessary to perform a mastec-
tomy. I was asked to call Steve and Jack Ford and tell them
of their mother's condition. Mike was there with us. We
managed to locate Jack and Steve out West. It was a difficult situation which tested everyone.

At the time, the President was involved in a major na-
tional economic conference in the nation's capital. When
the Saturday-afternoon session ended, he flew to the hospital to be with his wife. When the helicopter landed and
he came into the room, Jerry and I sat down and we
prayed briefly together. He asked me to read the verses I
had shared earlier with Betty. I've never seen him quite so
moved by anything as by Betty's surgery.

Later that night the family and I went to the White
House for dinner and then drove back to the hospital. We
did not know what to expect, so we quietly entered Betty's room. She cheerfully waved us in; the President's
relief was obvious. All of us were delighted and a bit
awed by her courage. That experience brought me closer
to the First Lady than ever before. Many, many times, I
would call the White House just to say hello to her and see
how she was doing. We could talk for forty-five minutes
or an hour. Usually we would close our conversation with
a quiet time of prayer. Although it isn't my habit to pray
with people on the telephone, the Fords made me feel at
ease and natural in doing it.

Our last visit to the White House was January 17, 1977.
The Fords were to move out in three days, but had invited
my entire family for a visit knowing how much it would
mean to Steve, Patti, and David. Jerry and I were alone in
the Oval Office, and we reminisced about many things.
Before I left, he said to me, "Billy, you've prayed for me in

this office many times. Now, let me pray for you." That's the memory I cherish of Jerry Ford as President. In his last few days in the White House, he was thinking, typically, not of what I could do for him, but what he could do for me.

We share many things in common, Jerry Ford and I, but the most significant bond between us is our love for Jesus Christ. He has seen the most powerful institutions of man, has been advised by this country's most brilliant intellectuals, has supervised its most complex and far-reaching programs—but Jerry Ford has never lost sight of the fact that God's got a better idea! Always and forever God *has* a better idea. I am so glad that I had a chance to be a part of this one!

God's Got a Better Idea

... *be bold and strong! Banish fear and doubt! For remember, the Lord your God is with you wherever you go.*

Joshua 1:9 LB

My Dear Father,

As I pray for strength and boldness, I pray for the wisdom to use them properly.

Remove not only fear and doubt, but their bedfellows of worry and anxiety.

Also, God, free me from the emotional turmoil that causes my stomach to need "Spiritual Tums,"

And may I never forget that because Your Son, Christ, is my Saviour,

Wherever I go, You go with me!

Dear God, may my life experience the peace of this verse this coming week.

In the Name of Jesus Christ, Your Son, my alive Saviour,

AMEN

Never forget to be truthful and kind. Hold these virtues tightly. Write them deep within your heart. If you want favor with both God and man, and a reputation for good judgment and common sense, then trust the Lord completely; don't ever trust in yourself. In everything you do, put God first, and he will direct you and crown your efforts with success.

Proverbs 3:3–6 LB

Dear God,

It is honest to admit that I want favor with men, that I want to be known for both common sense and good judgment.

But it is also true, my God, that I want favor with You because I am part of Your family through Your Son, Jesus Christ.

I ask You to allow me to have both favor with You and with my fellowman.

I want to put You first in my life and ask You to guide and direct me, and I will give You the honor for any success I achieve.

Bless those around me who have worked especially hard to help me achieve this honor.

May the marriage of truth and kindness be enhanced by the moving of Your Spirit in my life.

In Jesus' Name, AMEN

For I am not ashamed of this Good News about Christ. It is God's powerful method of bringing all who believe it to heaven. This message was preached first to the Jews alone, but now everyone is invited to come to God in this same way. This Good News tells us that God makes us ready for heaven—makes us right in God's sight—when we put our faith and trust in Christ to save us. This is accomplished from start to finish by faith. As the Scripture says it, "The man who finds life will find it through trusting God."

Romans 1:16, 17 LB

Dear God,

How thankful I am that I have the Good News that You make us ready for heaven when we put our faith in Your Son, Christ, to save us.

How grateful I am that I have done this.

Sometimes, God, it's hard to have faith because faith means we believe in Someone without seeing Him.

May my faith grow more and more as I trust in You.

Most of all, God, allow me not to be ashamed about my knowing Your Son as my Saviour.

May I be as excited about knowing Christ and sharing Him as I am about rooting for my favorite football team.

As I share Christ's Good News may it be just that to all who hear it!

In Jesus' Name, AMEN

But they that wait upon the Lord shall renew their strength. They shall mount up with wings like eagles; they shall run and not be weary; they shall walk and not faint.

Isaiah 40:31 LB

Dear God,

Teach me to wait.

It is so hard for me to wait.

God, may I not wait upon circumstance.

May I not wait upon people.

May I not wait upon plans.

May I wait upon You.

God, may I learn the difference between waiting upon You, and vacillating between men.

And from that waiting and because it is You I am waiting upon, may my strength be renewed.

May weariness of soul and faintness of heart not be a part of the vocabulary of my life.

But as my strength comes from You and the quality of my patience matures, may that strength of the eagle's wings give me the ability to soar—higher and higher and higher—

Until, with calmness of heart, I look over my problems and say,

"It has been good to wait upon You, my God. Thank you for being my source of strength. Teach me to wait on the Lord!"

In Jesus' Name, AMEN

And in every work that he began in the service of the house of God, and in the law, and in the commandments, to seek his God, he did it with all his heart, and prospered.

2 Chronicles 31:21 KJV

O God,

How do I learn to do things with all my heart?

Sometimes, Lord, I feel fainthearted, sometimes I feel halfhearted, sometimes I don't even care.

Yet, other times, I'm willing to give all I have.

God, teach me in every work that I do, to seek You and to give myself completely.

Keep me from being bugged by people who demand more of my time than I think they should have.

Keep me from developing a complacent attitude that says it's not worth 100 percent.

Give me the security that comes from You which allows me to say to my fellowman,

"I'll do it with all my heart!"

And to you, my God, may I say,

"I give all of my heart to seek You."

May I learn to prosper in God's sight, even though that prosperity is not always what it seems in man's sight.

God, You and I know that I am a Christian. May we both become pleased with the commitment of my heart to You and to my fellowman.

In the Name of Christ who gave His all, AMEN

Thy word have I hid in mine heart, that I might not sin against thee . . . . Thy word is a lamp unto my feet, and a light unto my path.

Psalms 119:11, 105 KJV

Dear God,

I hide many thoughts, many ideas, and many dreams deep inside my heart.

But God, let me learn to hide Your Word in my heart.

For if Your Word is there it will help me sift the good from the evil.

It will stop me from condoning things I do and say, and most important of all, it will pull me in the direction I need to go—toward You.

Your Son, Christ, is the light of the world and Your Word has the power to illuminate and clarify which way the path of righteousness leads.

May this prayer not just be repetitious rabble, but may I really learn Your Word and make it my word.

When temptations come, Lord, and we both know they will come, may my heart be so garrisoned by Your word that I face them in Your strength.

In the Name of Jesus Christ the Living Word of God,

AMEN

. . . for the Lord seeth not as man seeth; for man looketh on the outward appearance, but the Lord looketh on the heart.

1 Samuel 16:7 KJV

Dear God,

Help me not to judge someone too quickly or too harshly by that which appears to be obvious.

May I understand that other people see me and draw immediate conclusions.

Therefore, dear God, let my heartbeat for You be shown by my life—its actions and statements, both verbal and nonverbal.

Lord, You know me for You know my heart.

You see clearly through the outward facade and You know me.

May the man You know grow more and more to be the kind of man You want, and the kind of man You can use.

Help me keep my heart clean, for out of that heart comes the motivations of my life.

Teach me, God, to look beyond the apparent, beyond the obvious.

Help me to see people for what they are, what they can be, rather than what they appear to be.

God, in the responsibilities that I now have, may You be pleased as You look at my heart, and may I look at other people as You would look at them!

In Jesus' Name, AMEN

. . . Sir, we would see Jesus.
John 12:21 KJV

Dear God,

If there is ever a time of the year when people are aware of
Jesus, Your Son, it is now.
But God, do they really see Him?
Do they see who He really is?
Do they see what He came to do?
Do they see what He can be to them?
O God, may they see that Jesus is not just a baby in a
manger, that His meaning is not just the biggest
birthday party of all time, that His birthday does
not mean tinsel on the inside and tinsel on the
outside.
But how will people see Jesus?
Lord, most of them will not ask to see Him. Most people
will simply observe.
They will observe people like me, people who have seen
Him.
God, my prayer this season is that the real Jesus will be
seen in me!
Happy Birthday, Lord Jesus!

In Your Name, AMEN

O God, thou art my God; early will I seek thee . . . To see thy power and thy glory . . . . Because thy lovingkindness is better than life, my lips shall praise thee.

Psalms 63:1–3 KJV

Dear God,

You are infinitely perfect and worthy of infinite adoration.
I can offer no greater proof of my love than by presenting
    the worship that I owe.
This I willingly do from the depths of my being. See this
    worship.
Help me to offer it unceasingly until it becomes the nor-
    mal daily habit of my life.

In Jesus' precious Name, AMEN

But let a man examine himself . . . .
1 Corinthians 11:28 KJV

Gracious Lord,

Help me to examine myself
   to find out what virtues I lack,
      especially those that are hardest to acquire.
May I then, in perfect confidence, abide steadfast in Your
      presence
   asking for Your grace,
      finding Your strength,
         knowing Your power,
            and, in everything I attempt to do,

               Glorify Your wonderful Name! AMEN

Now when they saw the boldness . . . they marvelled;
and they took knowledge of them, that they had been with
Jesus.

Acts 4:13 KJV

Dear Lord,

I do not live in "normal" times.

I live among people who, via television, have seen the
world from the moon, but who are so uninformed
of *Thy* truth that they've never seen the world from
Heaven's vantage point.

So, this week, help me
To be enlightening—
To be inspirational—
To be nourishing—
To people who are hungry for hope based upon the truth
of God.

Let me say things of such value that the world would be
poorer if they were left unsaid.

Help me to help people to love You.

For Your glory, AMEN

Ask, and it shall be given you; seek, and ye shall find; knock, and it shall be opened unto you .
                                                            Matthew 7:7 KJV

Lord,

I face another busy, hectic week.
    Give me a sense of humor—the power to laugh.
Help me to do my homework—to be keenly observant.
    Make me uniquely qualified to stand tall.
Create in me a heart that is unafraid!
        Give me moments of quietness that I might enjoy
            Your presence, and
                Love You more!

                        In Jesus' Name, AMEN

Then was our mouth filled with laughter, and our tongue with singing: then said they among the heathen, The Lord hath done great things for them. The Lord hath done great things for us; whereof we are glad.

Psalms 126:2, 3 KJV

Lord,

Help me never, *even unconsciously,* to hide my love for my wonderful wife and four precious children.

They stand in the reflected glare of my public office and just by being my family endure pressures not experienced by other Americans.

Keep me mindful of their needs, with time to listen to their problems and sensitivity to be understanding, even when they don't bother to confide.

Thank You for these five treasures!

In Jesus' Name, AMEN

For God hath not given us the spirit of fear; but of power, and of love, and of a sound mind.

2 Timothy 1:7 KJV

Dear God,

Thank You for Your gifts!
    Though wonderfully blessed, I do face awesome responsibilities.
    Help me never to be afraid.
Let me grapple with the tasks of this week with an easy mind, confident of Your presence.
Fill every area of my life so that there is no room for failure
That always comes from within.
With Your strength in my life I *know* that I will be sufficient for each task.

In Jesus' Name I pray, AMEN

Many waters cannot quench the flame of love, neither can the floods drown it. If a man tried to buy it with everything he owned, he couldn't do it.

Song of Solomon 8:7 LB

Dear Lord,

I thank You for the consciousness that I am loved.
Loved by my family.
Loved by my friends.
Loved by a host of people whose names I do not know.
Most of all, I thank *You* that *You* love me!
Help me this week to keep my heart young and my eyes open so that nothing worthy of notice will escape me.
May I be cheerful in my contact with others and although the waters be swift, may they not put out the flame of love that You have put into my life.
Thank You for loving me just as I am!

I pray in the Name of Jesus Christ who loved me,
And gave Himself for me, AMEN

. . . in all these things we are more than conquerors through him that loved us.

Romans 8:37 KJV

Dear Lord,

That verse sounds extremely positive in light of the negative moments we have in our lives.

There are moments of difficulty that make this verse very hard to understand!

When we have smooth going and rapid progress, make me able to leave the good road for the rough way, where life is heavy and sometimes burdensome.

Let these detours teach me to be wise, and teach me to learn the importance of responding to people with greater energy.

Let the rough places that I face cause greater enthusiasm for fellowship with You.

May these rough places help me from falling into defeat.

Help me to learn to capitalize on the very high purposes which You have created within me as I serve You and people in this great land.

May Your love cause me to LIVE LOVE!

In Jesus' Name I pray, AMEN

*But God commendeth his love toward us, in that, while
we were yet sinners, Christ died for us.*

Romans 5:8 KJV

Dear God,

Why would You ever love me when I was so unworthy?
It is such good news that You care for and love those who
    are sinners.
Allow me this week to live as You would have me to
    live—to love all people, even in difficult situations.
Help me to stand for proper ideals,
   Help me to act to improve the lives of others,
    Help me to battle against injustice in every form.
Somehow, even though I am unworthy, let other people
    feel a ripple of love through my life.
Set me ablaze inside with a love for God and for people so
    that this love will warm Your heart as well as theirs.
I will not forget, dear God, that You loved me just as I was
    and, now, just as I am.
      May I do the same for other people!

In Jesus' Name, AMEN

He is not here: for he is risen . . . .
Matthew 28:6 KJV

Dear God,

What a great thought— to know that Your Son is not dead
in a Jerusalem grave, but alive in my heart!

Thank You, God, for this Easter season, and for allowing
me, through my trust in Your arisen Son, to be a
member of Your family.

May Your power—that overthrew the grave—cause me to
shout
"FOR ME TO LIVE IS CHRIST!"

May the problems I face daily be overpowered by the
resounding cry of
"CHRIST IS RISEN! HE IS RISEN INDEED!"

In Jesus' Name, AMEN

Call unto me, and I will answer thee, and shew thee
great and mighty things, which thou knowest not.

Jeremiah 33:3 KJV

Dear Lord,

At times everyone feels like they are being tested.
  Right now I feel as though I am being tested,
    and I need heavenly guidance for my earthly deeds
    as well as ultimate answers to immediate problems.
Help me to be properly related in a harmonious relation-
        ship to my family, my co-workers, and my
        friends—but most of all, dear Lord—
Keep me in a proper relationship with Your Son, the Lord
        Jesus Christ, who experienced the ultimate testing
        for me!

In the name of Your Son, Jesus, AMEN

*Come unto me, all ye that labour and are heavy laden,
and I will give you rest.*

Matthew 11:28 KJV

Dear God,

People are asking for rest, all kinds of rest—
   Rest for minds, rest for bodies, and rest for their spirits.
May I learn from You that the secret of rest is to come unto
      You.
It is not always easy to come to You because, often, I stand
      in the way.
   Pride, selfishness, and the desires of my heart block my
      way.
And, Lord, as I come unto You, may I learn more and
      more to allow people to come to me.
As You give me rest and peace and depth of soul may I do
      my best to meet the needs of those who come to
      me. May I accomplish this through Your strength
      and power.
Thank You for Your love-filled promise, "I will give you
      rest!"

In Jesus' Name, AMEN

Follow God's example in everything you do just as a much loved child imitates his father.

Ephesians 5:1 LB

Dear God,

I must admit that I look at people and sometimes try to follow their example but often I am let down.

My children follow me and I know at times they, too, are let down.

God, here it is plain and clear and straight from Your Word—I am to follow Your example.

This is hard for me to do because both of us know me really well. Yet, I am to follow You, God, as my leader.

Lord, I am not always sure that I will be able to follow You, but I will try.

This week as I face problems,

       people with needs,

       and people who may be against me,

May I not only follow Your example, but may I follow the principles You have lovingly stated for me to follow.

God, I thank You that I will be better able to lead men, as I follow You!

In Jesus' Name, AMEN

. . . Much is required from those to whom much is given, for their responsibility is greater.

Luke 12:48 LB

Lord,

Sometimes I like to think I am very talented and that I have a lot to offer.

Yet, when I read Your Word, Lord, and see this verse, I back off.

Because if I do have some talent—even a little bit—I will be required to use it properly.

Thank You, Lord, for a verse like this that helps me to balance myself.

Whatever talents You have given me, Lord, I want to be responsible to You for them.

I want to use these talents well for Your honor and Your glory.

Do not let me be double-minded, Lord,

talking big about talent when there is no price to pay, and then slacking off when I realize that I will be held accountable.

God, You really have a way of making me face myself. Thanks for this!

In Jesus' Name, AMEN

His lord said unto him, Well done, good and faithful servant; thou hast been faithful over a few things, I will make thee ruler over many things: enter thou into the joy of thy lord.

Matthew 25:23 KJV

Lord,

Please help me to be faithful.
You know how much I appreciate it **when** people say to me, "Well done! Good job!"
O God, it would make my life on earth worthwhile, if someday You will say to me, "Well done, good and faithful servant!"
God, help me to be faithful even in the small things I do.
Teach me to be faithful, not just to people or principles—
Help me, Lord, to be ever faithful to You.

Through faith in Christ, AMEN

Tears came to Jesus' eyes.
John 11:35 LB

Dear God,

Let me be compassionate.

Let me be able to see the needs of people and let those
needs move me.

May I be the kind of man who can weep—not afraid to cry,
not afraid that I will ruin some false image.

May I realize that You cried—because You cared!

Please help me to avoid becoming hardened, O Lord,
even to the little things.

Teach me to be sensitive—sensitive enough, if need be, to
cry—and then, for Your sake, to do something
about the need.

In Jesus' Name, AMEN

Finally, my brethren, be strong in the Lord, and in the power of his might. Put on the whole armour of God, that ye may be able to stand against the wiles of the devil.

Ephesians 6:10 KJV

Dear Lord,

I am being pulled in many directions.
    I am being stretched tight.
        Everywhere I go, people demand attention.
Help me to face my limitations and hold me together with
        an inward peace—a peace that will keep me steady
        under pressure.
Give depth to my speech and significance to my actions.
In a trying hour, let *me* be *Your* man.

In Jesus' Name, AMEN

*And you will know the truth, and the truth will set
you free.*

John 8:32 LB

Dear Lord,

Everyone seems to be searching for truth today.
Perhaps more than any other time in my life, I am aware
of how important truth is.
Teach me to know more than surface truth—that I may
face the realization that YOU ARE TRUTH. Lord,
You are the ultimate truth!
As I develop my values through You, Your truth shall
make me free.
I shall be free from confusion.
I shall be free from the constant pecking away of human
doubt.
I shall be free from the insecurity of not knowing
which way to go.
God, I thank You that I know You. May Your truth not
only march on through me—but may it penetrate
the very essence of my being!

In Jesus' Name, AMEN

*Once when Jesus had been out praying, one of his disci-
ples came to him as he finished and said, "Lord, teach us a
prayer . . . ."*

Luke 11:1 LB

O Lord,

What a prayer to pray to You!
> I am praying to You to ask You, Lord, to teach me to pray.
> Lord, I need to know not only how to pray but how to pray regularly.

Sometimes it is my fault that I do not pray. If I would only begin to pray—prayer would come easier.

When I realize that YOU ARE ALMIGHTY GOD, and I am just another human being, another of Your Creations, it is very hard for me to come before You.

It is only when I stop to realize that because of my belief in Your Son, Jesus Christ, You consider me important—that I can come to You, and come more often.

I ask You to help me to come to You more in prayer.
> TEACH ME, LORD! TEACH ME TO PRAY!

In Jesus' Name, AMEN

Oh, that these men would praise the Lord for his lovingkindness, and for all of his wonderful deeds! For he satisfies the thirsty soul and fills the hungry soul with good.

Psalms 107:8, 9 LB

Lord,

It has become so easy just to sit and complain.

It has become so easy to become a junior prophet of doom.

Yet, how silly to do so, when I think of all the blessings and all the goodness of God.

Lord, I want to praise You now for all You have given me, for all that You are.

When I face it, Lord, it is You who satisfies my soul.

It is You, Lord, who fills the vacuum inside of me.

Lord, forgive me for being negative.

Accept, now, my praise and thanks for being so wonderful!

In Jesus' Name, AMEN

But Jesus the Son of God is our great High Priest who has gone to heaven itself to help us; therefore let us never stop trusting him. This High Priest of ours understands our weaknesses, since he had the same temptations we do, though he never once gave way to them and sinned. So let us come boldly to the very throne of God and stay there to receive his mercy and to find grace to help us in our times of need.

Hebrews 4:14–16 LB

Dear Lord,

Thank You, Lord!

You always make me feel welcome when I stop to pray.

Sometimes I'm burdened with cares—wearily I move ahead.

Often, Lord, I am frightened.

When I commit my way to You, I am no longer afraid.

What a comfort to know that You care and that You answer prayer.

Make this week unfold to Your glory.

In Jesus' Name, AMEN

*. . . I want to remind you that your strength must come
from the Lord's mighty power within you.*

Ephesians 6:10 LB

Dear God,

It is so good of You to remind me of important matters in
many different ways, but especially through Your
Word.

There are times when I feel very weak, times when I feel
strong.

There are times when I feel capable of attacking any problem that my leadership demands.

Then there are times when the burden of responsibility
becomes overpowering.

Father, whether it be moments of weakness or moments
of strength, may I realize that my strength does
come from Your mighty power within me.

Thank You for reminding me of this truth.

Help me to relax in the calmness and security that I can do
all things through Christ whose mighty power is
working in me.

Because I know myself, I'll need reminding again—that
my strength is in the Lord.

Remind me again, Lord.

In Jesus' Name, AMEN

This is what I have asked of God for you: that you will be encouraged and knit together by strong ties of love, and that you will have the rich experience of knowing Christ with real certainty and clear understanding. For God's secret plan, now at last made known, is Christ himself. *In him lie hidden all the mighty, untapped treasures of wisdom and knowledge.*

I am saying this because I am afraid that someone may fool you with smooth talk. For though I am far away from you my heart is with you, happy because you are getting along so well, happy because of your strong faith in Christ. And now just as you trusted Christ to save you, trust him, too, for each day's problems; live in vital union with him. Let your roots grow down into him and draw up nourishment from him. See that you go on growing in the Lord, and become strong and vigorous in the truth you were taught. Let your lives overflow with joy and thanksgiving for all he has done.

Don't let others spoil your faith and joy with their philosophies, their wrong and shallow answers built on men's thoughts and ideas, instead of on what Christ has said. For in Christ there is all of God in a human body; so you have everything when you have Christ, *and you are filled with God through your union with Christ. He is the highest Ruler, with authority over every other power.*

Colossians 2:2–10 LB

Dear God,

You have said it clearly.
    You have said it well.
        Help me to live it!

In Jesus' Name, AMEN

If we are living now by the Holy Spirit's power, let us follow the Holy Spirit's leading in every part of our lives. Then we won't need to look for honors and popularity, which lead to jealousy and hard feelings.

Galatians 5:25, 26 LB

Father,

I know that I should let the Spirit of God be the power in my life. Then it would be easy to follow His leading.

But, Lord, when You say in *every* part of my life, that takes in some pretty rough situations. And then again, You and I are the only two who honestly know about these areas, therefore, my inner failures are no real surprise to You. In spite of knowing them, You still love me and want to lead me.

Sometimes I look for honors and popularity, and sometimes my motivation is wrong.

Maybe that's what brings the jealousy and hard feelings.

But if I don't look for popularity and honor and You give them to me because You choose to, then people seem to accept it.

Help me to follow the Holy Spirit's leading—not looking out of personal ambition but accepting that which He gives to me.

Thanks an awful lot for considering *me* worthwhile enough to even bother to lead.

Really, God, You do amaze me!

In Jesus' Name, AMEN

There is a right time for everything:

A time to be born,	*A time to die;*
A time to plant;	*A time to harvest;*
A time to kill;	*A time to heal;*
A time to destroy;	*A time to rebuild;*
A time to cry;	*A time to laugh;*
A time to grieve;	*A time to dance;*
A time for scattering stones;	*A time for gathering stones;*
A time to hug;	*A time not to hug;*
A time to find;	*A time to lose;*
A time for keeping;	*A time for throwing away;*
A time to tear;	*A time to repair;*
A time to be quiet;	*A time to speak up;*
A time for loving;	*A time for hating;*
A time for war;	*A time for peace.*

Ecclesiastes 3:1–8 LB

Lord,

Many times each day I say, "What time is it?"

As I look at this passage of Scripture, Father, I say, "What time is it?"

Lord, allow me to do the right thing at the right time.

Help me to be so close to You that I will *know* what time it is.

Your Son came to us in the fullness of Your time.

May my life reflect the proper usage of the fullness of time.

In Jesus' Name, AMEN

Your attitude should be the kind that was shown us by Jesus Christ, who, though he was God, did not demand and cling to his rights as God, but laid aside his mighty power and glory, taking the disguise of a slave and becoming like men. And he humbled himself even further, going so far as actually to die a criminal's death on a cross.

Yet it was because of this that God raised him up to the heights of heaven and gave him a name which is above every other name, that at the name of Jesus every knee shall bow in heaven and on earth and under the earth, and every tongue shall confess that Jesus Christ is Lord, to the glory of God the Father.

Philippians 2:5–11 LB

Dear Lord,

Sometimes it is so very hard not to demand and cling to that which I think I deserve and that which seems rightfully mine.

But when I think, Father, that Your Son gave up His very right as God and laid that right aside in order to die a criminal's death on a cross for me, then I understand what it means truly to humble myself.

Help me, Lord, not always to fight for what I feel I deserve—and often don't.

Help me, Lord, to think of my responsibilities as well as my rights.

May I be grateful that I have already bowed my knee and opened my heart to You and to Your Son, Christ Jesus.

Thank you, Father, for what Your Son, Christ, has done for me.

May the attitude that He had, be the attitude that controls my inner life as well as my outward dealings with people, even those people, Lord, who, for me, aren't too lovable.

In Jesus' Name, AMEN

If you can find a truly good wife, she is worth more than precious gems! Her husband can trust her, and she will richly satisfy his needs. She will not hinder him, but help him all her life . . . .

She is a woman of strength and dignity, and has no fear of old age. When she speaks, her words are wise, and kindness is the rule for everything she says. She watches carefully all that goes on throughout her household, and is never lazy. Her children stand and bless her; so does her husband. He praises her with these words: "There are many fine women in the world, but you are the best of them all!"

Charm can be deceptive and beauty doesn't last, but a woman who fears and reverences God shall be greatly praised. Praise her for the many fine things she does. These good deeds of hers shall bring her honor and recognition from even the leaders of the nations.

Proverbs 31:10–12, 25–31 LB

Dear God,

I have thanked You for many things, but at times I have forgotten to thank You for the person on this earth who means the most to me—My Beloved.

Lord, one day we said to each other, ". . . in sickness and in health . . . ."

Through Your love that promise has become a living commitment.

Help me to show and to share my love.

Thank You for giving me one *without* whom my life would have been lonely and *with* whom my life has been worthwhile!

In Jesus' Name, AMEN

*A man is a fool to trust himself! But those who use God's
wisdom are safe.*

Proverbs 28:26 LB

Dear God,

Help me to realize that Your wisdom is that which I
should seek after.

Teach me the principles of good judgment and common
sense.

Instill in me the longing to seek after You, and help me to
avoid the trap of trusting myself above that which
You have taught me.

May I be wise in Your sight, and may men realize that my
wisdom comes from You.

In Jesus' Name, AMEN

But God is so rich in mercy; he loved us so much that even though we were spiritually dead and doomed by our sins, he gave us back our lives again when he raised Christ from the dead—only by his undeserved favor have we ever been saved—and lifted us up from the grave into glory along with Christ, where we sit with him in the heavenly realms—all because of what Christ Jesus did.

Ephesians 2:4–6 LB

God,

As I read these verses I realize that I am undeserving of Your forgiveness.

I also realize that it was Your gracious mercy that brought Christ to the cross, to the grave, and, gratefully, from the empty tomb, to save me from my guilt and sin.

O God, I am astonished when I think of the person I could be if only I would allow the truth of Your Resurrection to come alive in me.

I am thankful that You are rich in mercy, so rich that there is enough mercy FOR EVERYONE IN THE WORLD IF THEY SIMPLY BELIEVE IN YOUR SON, CHRIST!

Help me share that merciful forgiveness of what You have done for men and women everywhere.

In Jesus' Name, AMEN

*I have thought much about your words, and stored them
in my heart so that they would hold me back from sin.*

Psalms 119:11 LB

Dear God,

Help me to realize the authority and power of the Scriptures.

Help me to realize that the Word of God is the base for my life—not only morally, but intellectually as well.

Help me to take time to hide the Word of God in my heart—

so I can draw upon its resources,

so I can refill my own life by its power,

so it will always be with me,

That through the Word of God I might find the strength I need to face my job.

You have given me a high office.

May the power and strength of the Word of God make me ever aware of my responsibilities to my fellowman and to You.

Help me, Lord, to live a life that represents my Christian belief, powerfully.

In Jesus' Name, AMEN

His lord said unto him, Well done, good and faithful servant; thou hast been faithful over a few things, I will make thee ruler over many things: enter thou into the joy of thy lord.

Matthew 25:23 KJV

Lord,

It seems that the word *faithful* runs through Your Word
so much—

> Faithful to You
> Faithful to my wife
> Faithful to my family
> Faithful to my friends
> Faithful to my country
> Faithful to my belief in the Christian philosophy

Father, here You ask me to be faithful over a few things,
even some small things.

In all honesty, sometimes it is very hard to be faithful. Yet
when I am faithful over these small things, You put
me over many things.

Thank You for Your faithfulness to me, O Lord. Forgive
me for my neglect in not thanking You for Your
greatness.

I want to enter into the joys of the Lord and have the
happiness of Yourself in my heart.

I want to be a good and faithful servant to You.

In Jesus' Name, AMEN

Commit thy works unto the Lord, and thy thoughts shall be established.

Proverbs 16:3 KJV

Father,

Sometimes it is very hard to commit what I am doing unto
    You.
If I can only realize that if I will do this—
    You will help me to establish
        the thoughts
        the thought patterns
        the ideas
        the creativeness
I need to handle properly the problems that life brings to
    me.
Why should it be hard to commit my works to You?
I have already committed my soul to You, Lord.
I have already committed my life to You, Lord.
I need Your help in committing the very works of my
    daily schedule into Your hands.
Thank You, God, for accepting my commitment. Help me
    to share with others the importance of a total com-
    mitment to You.

In Jesus' Name, AMEN

. . . God was in Christ, reconciling the world unto him-self . . . .

2 Corinthians 5:19 KJV

Father,

I cannot read this passage of Scripture without being awed at the fact that—
>You, Almighty God, were in Christ
>>As He was born in a manger,
>>As He died on that cross,
>>As He arose from the dead.

To think that I can be reconciled to You, the great God of the Universe, is too much to comprehend.

I thank You, God, for reconciling me unto Yourself.

Help me to be a man that causes people to be reconciled to each other.

Help me in the world in which I live to share the fact that Christ can reconcile people unto Himself, and that reconciliation will bring
>Peace on earth and goodwill toward men!

In Jesus' Name, AMEN

If you love someone you will be loyal to him no matter what the cost. You will always believe in him, always expect the best of him, and always stand your ground in defending him.

1 Corinthians 13:7 LB

Dear God,

In a time of history when true love and true loyalty are hard to find, I look at Your Word and find a clear pattern.

In Your Word, Lord, there are proofs of love.

May I evidence those proofs of love to those around me.

Teach me to be able to discern, Lord, those people who really love me and the ones who are truly loyal to me.

Help me to know those who double-talk, those who feign loyalty on one hand, but are motivated impurely on the other.

Give me love. Give me loyalty. Teach me to stand for those about whom I care.

Develop in me a sensitivity that allows me to discern true love and true loyalty in those who are important to what I am, and what I do.

In Jesus' Name, AMEN

For unto us a child is born, unto us a son is given . . . .
Isaiah 9:6 KJV

Dear God,

For a year now we've said You've had a better idea.
  This very week is the evidence of that better idea.
Your Son was given unto us in the form of a child, born as a child.
We celebrate this day, the birthday of the child, but we also realize that the Son of God is eternal.
As He lived, died upon a cross, and rose from the dead—
  that Babe in a manger became the Risen Saviour.
At this season may we reaffirm the fact that only through our trust and faith in this Jesus may we have the one gift that surpasses all—
    The gift of eternal life as a member of "God's Forever Family."
We know that if the Son was not given, Your only begotten Son, a child could not have been born.
We do not bow our heads to coo at a baby in swaddling clothes in a manger—
We lift our eyes to Heaven where Your Son, Christ, sits at Your right hand.
We say to You,
    "Thank You, Sir, for Your unspeakable gift.
    May we not only accept Him but serve Him with all our hearts!"
In the Name of Jesus, the Son that was given, and the baby that was born,

AMEN

It is a badge of honor to accept valid criticism.
Proverbs 25:12 LB

Dear God,

The hardest thing for me to figure out about criticism is its
validity.
Is it truth—or is somebody bugged at me?
Is it something about me—or something I do that bugs
them?
Or—are they really talking about the issue?
I really don't like to be criticized unless it can help.
Teach me to accept criticism and then discern if it is valid
or not.
God, You have done so much for me.
You can keep the badge—if I can grow enough to
understand its principle.

In Jesus' Name, AMEN

Now therefore, I pray thee, if I have found grace in thy sight, shew me now thy way, that I may know thee, that I may find grace in thy sight: and consider that this nation is thy people.

Exodus 33:13 KJV

Dear God,

You have been good to me! You have showed me so much of Your grace already.

Now I need to know Your way. I also want to know You in a deeper way.

God, I have a great responsibility
    to You,
    to myself,
    to this Nation.

I pray wholeheartedly and sincerely that this Nation is Thy people.

Although we have not always acted as Your people and often disgust You with things we do and say—Your forgiving power is great.

I pray that this Nation, beginning with me, starts to show evidence that
    WE REALLY WANT TO BE PEOPLE WHO
    ARE LED AND DIRECTED BY GOD.

Encourage those who stand true and strong.
    Assist those who fall lame and weak.

And Lord, give me the grace and the knowledge and the wisdom to lead these, Thy people.

In Jesus' Name, AMEN

Wounds from a friend are better than kisses from an enemy.

Proverbs 27:6 LB

Father,

It is unpleasant for me to be wounded.

> Whether the wound is physical, emotional, mental, or spiritual, it always hurts.

If a friend loves me, cares about me, and tells me something for my own benefit that wounds me,

> > May I then accept that wound as constructive—
> >
> > Accept the feeling of sorrow—
> >
> > And *learn the lesson of instruction.*

Teach me also, Father, to be aware of my enemies and their flattering kisses, the kisses of pretense.

You are my best friend, Father, and I realize that the wounds You allow are for my own benefit.

> Help me to accept constructive wounds.

In Jesus' Name, AMEN

Reverence for God gives a man deep strength; his children have a place of refuge and security.

Reverence for the Lord is a fountain of life; its waters keep a man from death.

Proverbs 14:26, 27 LB

Lord,

Some of the simplest things escape us.

My actions and my basic philosophy say that I have great Reverence for You.

Father, is this really true of me?

You have impressed upon me by these Scripture verses the importance of having real Reverence for You.

The inner strength that I need and must have—the source of life that must come from me—can come from Reverence for You.

Father, my children will never have that place of Reverence and security, if they do not see the example of it in me.

You are worth much more in my finite Reverence but I give it to You with all my heart!

In Jesus' Name, AMEN

Kind words are like honey—enjoyable and healthful.
                              Proverbs 16:24 LB

Father,

With all of the sourness and tartness in today's world,
    help *my* words to be words like honey.
May they be sweet and honest.
May I commend and bless in such a way that the results
    are enjoyable and healthful.
Cause me to realize, Lord, that kind words are not always
    words that sound kind.
Sometimes kind words reprimand while at other times
    they are a soft disagreement.
May I understand that kind words must come out of a
    heart that has kindness in it.
Give me the right kind of kindness in my heart to put
    forth the right kind of words.

                              In Jesus' Name, AMEN

Love forgets mistakes; nagging about them parts the best of friends.

Proverbs 17:9 LB

Lord,

It is so easy to remember mistakes and so hard to forgive the mistakes of others.

If love is in control, it will cause me to forget and forgive those mistakes.

Lord, I need also to forget my own mistakes.

Help me not to have guilt feelings for doing wrong. Remind me to ask Your forgiveness and then forgive myself—as You have forgiven me.

May I not be one who nags or is a constant source of negation—causing those around me to want to leave my company.

Help me to be one, Lord, who not only forgets mistakes, but works to build up the people around me in such a way that through Your strength shown in my life they will be drawn closer to You, rather than farther away.

Help this prayer, O Lord, to be an action prayer in my daily existence.

In Jesus' Name, AMEN

But the angel said, "Don't be so surprised. Aren't you looking for Jesus, the Nazarene who was crucified? He isn't here! He has come back to life! Look, that's where his body was lying. Now go and give this message to his disciples including Peter:

" 'Jesus is going ahead of you to Galilee. You will see him there, just as he told you before he died!' "

Mark 16:6, 7 LB

Dear Lord,

How could the angel say, "including Peter"?

> This Peter who denied Christ three times—
> This man, who did not really believe the Resurrection was coming—
> This man whose life in the last minutes of Christ's life, was against Christ.

How could the angel say, "including Peter"?

Then I stop and think, Lord, that often *I* am the one who is Peter.

> *I* am the one who because of the sin in my life, because of my attitude or my action, turns against You, and You always say to me, "including Peter."

Thank You most of all for being able to say, "including Peter," and for letting that Peter be me.

In Jesus' Name, AMEN

Jesus saith unto him, I am the way, the truth, and the life: no man cometh unto the Father, but by me.

John 14:6 KJV

Dear God,

No man could make that statement unless he be of You. In fact, only Your Son could make that statement.

When I try to comprehend that Jesus, Himself, is the sum of
> THE WAY
> THE TRUTH
> THE LIFE—

It makes me realize my need to look to Him for direction.
> *I need to look to Him!*

As Christ is the light of the world, I am to be a light for Him.

May I also point men to Him
> by being THE WAY to men by my life-style,
> by being THE TRUTH by my sincere integrity,
> and by being THE LIFE by the breath of His Spirit in me.

In Jesus' Name, AMEN

Every morning tell him, "Thank you for your kindness,"
and every evening rejoice in his faithfulness.

Psalms 92:2 LB

Dear God,

What a simple request.

How little time it would take to do what is asked in this
verse.

It seems so easy to make this prayer, a prayer of
thanksgiving for Your kindness, a prayer of rejoicing for Your faithfulness.

Lord, help me to apply more than just the theory of this
verse.

Help me to actually pray the kind of prayer Your words
suggest.

Be with me in my relationship to others so that I balance
thanksgiving for kindness and rejoicing for faithfulness.

Remind me, O God, to talk to You each morning and
evening and—

"Thank You for Your kindness!"

In Jesus' Name, AMEN

When I look up into the night skies and see the work of your fingers—the moon and the stars you have made—I cannot understand how you can bother with mere puny man, to pay any attention to him!

Psalms 8:3, 4 LB

Father,

As I walk alone at night and look up into the sky and see
   the stars,
   the moon,
   the cloud formations,
  and realize how small this earth really is, it stuns
   me!
Then I try to comprehend how small *I am*
   on this very small planet,
   in a very small solar system,
   in the vast universe.
How can You even be interested in me enough to hear my
   prayers?
How can You be concerned about the plan for my life?
How can You be concerned about the feelings of my soul?
And yet You are.
And it amazes me even more to know that Jesus Christ
   came to this little planet to redeem puny little me.
Thank You, God, for making me significant, and for pay-
   ing such a price to do so.

In Jesus' Name, AMEN

A man who refuses to admit his mistakes can never be successful . . . .

Proverbs 28:13 LB

Father,

Who would be ignorant enough not to admit mistakes?
Yet, Lord, sometimes I realize that this verse is in the Bible for a reason.
Thank You for this verse.
Lord, it immediately stops me from beginning a pattern of being afraid to say I'm wrong.
To become Your child, I had to admit my mistakes and my own unworthiness and sinfulness.
Now I can experience not only the joy of forgiveness from You, but I am able to face myself as an imperfect person—knowing that You love me anyway.
May I not be afraid to show my imperfections to others.

In Jesus' Name, AMEN

Always be joyful.
　　1 Thessalonians 5:16 LB

Lord,

When I first read this verse I felt like saying, "You've got
　　to be kidding!" *Always* is a powerful word.
How am I to be joyful?
　　　　　Do You mean joyful inside?
　　　　　Do You mean a joyful spirit?
　　　　　Do You mean joyful outwardly?
　　　　　Do You mean joyful actions?
The truth of this verse is that You are right—but then, *You
　　are God.*
Remember, I am human.
I'll give it my best if You will help me.

　　　　　　　　　　In Jesus' Name, AMEN

My times are in thy hand . . . .
Psalms 31:15 KJV

Father,

As time passes for me on this earth I realize more and
more that not only is my time in Your hands, my
life is in Your hands.

You have allowed me the ability to make decisions, the
ability to think.

And yet, as God, You are more than just there—
You are alert, alive, responsible.

Thank You for being the kind of God that has not just let
me stagger around this earth as some unknown
computerized number.

Thank You for enabling me to commit to You my very
being, knowing that You care and that Your concern is not only for my time here on earth—which
is of importance to me now—but for my time in
Heaven—which is to come.

In Jesus' Name, AMEN

But I would not have you to be ignorant, brethren, concerning them which are asleep, that ye sorrow not, even as others which have no hope.

For if we believe that Jesus died and rose again, even so them also which sleep in Jesus will God bring with him.

For this we say unto you by the word of the Lord, that we which are alive and remain unto the coming of the Lord shall not prevent them which are asleep.

For the Lord himself shall descend from heaven with a shout, with the voice of the archangel, and with the trump of God: and the dead in Christ shall rise first:

Then we which are alive and remain shall be caught up together with them in the clouds, to meet the Lord in the air: and so shall we ever be with the Lord.

Wherefore comfort one another with these words.

1 Thessalonians 4:13–18 KJV

Lord,

What a frightening phrase, God, "Sorrow not, even as others which have no hope."

I realize, Christ, that if You had not died upon the cross, been buried, and risen again from the dead for my sins,

I WOULD HAVE NO HOPE.

My hope is also in Your Second Coming.

You will someday come back again, to take me with You, forever.

Lord, that is almost too much for me to comprehend!

Thanks, God, for giving me hope, HOPE through Your Son, and the realization that

You actually want to have me with You, forever.

In Jesus' Name, AMEN

Anxious hearts are very heavy, but a word of encouragement does wonders!

Proverbs 12:25 LB

Father,

There are times that all of us become anxious.
There are times when we all feel a heaviness in our souls.
We should know better, but it happens to all of us.
Dear God, help me to be one that encourages others,
not simply for the benefit of lifting them up,
but with the hope of teaching myself the lesson
that the end result of anxiousness is usually negative.
Thank *You* for being *my* encouragement!

In Jesus' Name, AMEN

The path of the godly leads to life. So why fear death?
Proverbs 12:28 LB

Dear God,

One of the things I really like about You is that You think
long-term.
I know this verse means more than life on earth—it refers
to life after death.
You are logical, God:
>Why should I fear death if it does not end
>life—if it begins Eternal Life?
But Lord, You and I know that when that plane bounces
in turbulent weather,
>when my car skids across the ice,
>when I cannot reach my wife for hours on the tele-
>phone,
>when my children do not return when they are
>supposed to,
>I DO FEAR.
Lord, maybe I should be more godly. Sir, with Your help,
I will try.

In Jesus' Name, AMEN

You are living a brand new kind of life that is continually learning more and more of what is right, and trying constantly to be more and more like Christ who created this new life within you. In this new life one's nationality or race or education or social position is unimportant; such things mean nothing. Whether a person has Christ is what matters, and he is equally available to all.

Colossians 3:10, 11 LB

Father,

Sometimes I use the excuse that anything brand new is hard to learn and thus avoid the simplicity of these verses.

Help me to learn more and more to *be* and *do* what is right.

Help me to pattern myself to be more like Your Son, Christ.

May my priorities be adjusted so that the most important factor in my life, or anyone's life, is to know Christ as Saviour.

Teach me to avoid the trappings of man's status symbols.

May I, through my conversation, assure men that Your Son is equally available to all men who believe in Him.

In Jesus' Name, AMEN

Let everyone be sure that he is doing his very best, for then he will have the personal satisfaction of work well done, and won't need to compare himself with someone else. Each of us must bear some faults and burdens of his own. For none of us is perfect!

Galatians 6:4, 5 LB

Father,

I wonder how often I work and do things out of guilt
—You know, don't You?
I wonder how often I try to achieve something for You
when I am really trying to "overachieve" someone
else
—You know, don't You?
Sometimes I strive for personal satisfaction without realizing that satisfaction can be supplied by doing my best and completely fulfilling my responsibilities.
Father, I am glad you have offered me the possibility of failure because we all have faults.
I am happy that Your Word allows for my nonperfection.
Lord, help me avoid a rigid complex of perfection, yet help me balance this with a high goal to do my best.
Teach me to be happy that I am myself and that "par for the course" is not beating someone else, but playing against my own assets and liabilities.
It's just like You not to put pressure on me, but lovingly to strengthen me and urge me to move on!
—You know, don't You?

In Jesus' Name, AMEN

May God who gives patience, steadiness, and encour-
agement help you to live in complete harmony with each
other—each with the attitude of Christ toward the other.
                                   Romans 15:5 LB

Dear Lord,

You have described a situation in this verse that would be
    ideal.

If I lived the attitude of Christ all the time, and my brother
    lived the same attitude, we would have complete
    harmony.

But, Lord, You especially know how very human I am,
    and that often my attitudes are not right.

I am accountable to You for my attitudes and my actions,
    and I pray that You will help me to live the attitude
    of Christ in my relationships with people.

May this especially be true in my relationship with my
    wife and children.

                              In Jesus' Name, AMEN

But as for you, speak up for the right living that goes along with true Christianity.

Titus 2:1 LB

Father,

You tell me to speak up. Do You realize how difficult it is for me to speak up?

It is hard enough for me to "flesh out" the right kind of living, and to speak up for it *really* puts me on the line.

Father, teach me to balance the need for speaking and the need for living.

Give me the wisdom to do so in a manner that presents Christianity as the Truth.

In Jesus' Name, AMEN

> *Let him have all your worries and cares, for he is always*
> *thinking about you and watching everything that concerns*
> *you.*
>
> 1 Peter 5:7 LB

Father,

When I read this verse I breathe a sigh of relief because,
   theoretically, it is fantastic.
   The problem is not with You.
   The problem is with me.
I am not always able to release the worries and concerns
   that I have, nor am I able to comprehend the fact
   that You are watching *everything* that concerns me.
How much easier life would be and how much less pres-
   sure I would be under if I were able to experience
   this verse daily.
Thank You for putting this verse in the Bible, and thank
   You for its meaning.
   I pray that I will practice it more and more.

In Jesus' Name, AMEN

The whole Bible was given to us by inspiration from God and is useful to teach us what is true and to make us realize what is wrong in our lives; it straightens us out and helps us do what is right. It is God's way of making us well prepared at every point, fully equipped to do good to everyone.

2 Timothy 3:16, 17 LB

Lord,

There it is—clear and understandable.
The Word of God is Your Book and has in it the principles
        to teach me what is true,
        to straighten me out,
        to show me what is wrong in my life.
I believe this, Lord. You know I do.
But why, then, do I have so much trouble in taking time
        to open the Bible and to read it?
I need to be reminded that if I read Your Word more, I
        would be better prepared and equipped for daily
        life.
        Father, I will try to read it and live it more.

In Jesus' Name, AMEN

Keep your eyes open for spiritual danger; stand true to the Lord; act like men; be strong; and whatever you do, do it with kindness and love.

1 Corinthians 16:13, 14 LB

Father,

We often think of danger—physical danger, emotional danger, financial danger—but we seldom really concentrate on the fact that there is spiritual danger.

Help me to be aware that there are those philosophies, ideas, and conducts that would endanger my relationship with You.

Father, may I balance that defense of being alert for spiritual danger, with the offense of standing, acting, being, and doing.

Give me the balance, Lord, of welding these two thoughts.

In Jesus' Name, AMEN

It is better to eat soup with someone you love than steak with someone you hate.

Proverbs 15:17 LB

Dear God,

Keep my values straight and—when they drift—help me bring them back, dead center.

Father, it is important for me to understand the great worth of those who love me, and not to be awed by position, possession, or the things of this world.

Teach me not to sacrifice commitment to people and my beliefs in order to get something "special."

In Jesus' Name, AMEN

A person who is pure of heart sees goodness and purity in everything; but a person whose own heart is evil and untrusting finds evil in everything, for his dirty mind and rebellious heart color all he sees and hears.

Titus 1:15 LB

Dear God,

Really, now, it is awfully hard to see goodness and purity
    in everything.
        But, then, how pure is *my* heart?
God, I know my views are colored—
        by my own motivation,
        by my own mind,
        by my own philosophies.
Father, help that base to be pure.

In Jesus' Name, AMEN

Stop listening to teaching that contradicts what you know is right.

Proverbs 19:27 LB

Lord,

Your Word has taught me certain principles, a base upon which to build my life.

Yet, sometimes, I hear ideas and concepts that sound interesting, and, occasionally, they make sense even though I know they are against what You have said is Truth.

Father, help me only to *know* what is right, but to *be* what is right.

In Jesus' Name, AMEN

For unto us a child is born, unto us a son is given . . . .
                                        Isaiah 9:6 KJV

Dear God,

On this Christmas day, year after year,
        we celebrate,
        we holiday,
        we party,
        we stuff ourselves,
        we give,
        we receive,
        we decorate trees,
        we hang stockings,
        we kiss under mistletoe,
        we divide our presents into three groups—those we
        keep, those we exchange, and those we give to
        someone else next year.
None of these are wrong in themselves; some are even beauti-
    ful.
Yet if they become paramount, we blindly miss the real mean-
    ing of this day.
Sometimes, Father, we go overboard about the "Child."
May we realize that Christ was born not just to coo at—lying in
    swaddling clothes in a manger in Bethlehem or a plastic
    crib in Grand Rapids.
Christ is Your Son given to us, placed by You in a human family
    to serve, to live, to die on a cross, and to come alive
    again.
Thank You for this unutterable gift. He is what Christmas is all
    about.
Help us to enjoy all the expressions of Christmas,
    but may we wholly comprehend at this season that through
    our trust in Him
      we have the one gift that surpasses all others—the gift of
      belonging—belonging to God as a member of His
      "Forever Family."
Thank You, God, for caring so much.
        In the Name of Jesus, the Son that was given and the
        Child that was born,

                                              AMEN

Fear not, for I am with you. Do not be dismayed. I am your God. I will strengthen you; I will help you . . . .
Isaiah 41:10 LB

Father,

As we look ahead to a year of uncertainty, a year of doubts, it is reassuring to know that You are my God.

Father, it overwhelms me that YOU are *my* God!

The God of Creation is my own God!

Stay with me, Father, even though at times I am sure I am trying.

I pray that You will continue to strengthen and help me.

At the beginning of this new year I pledge You my love.

I desire to live that love for You
in my daily relationships with people.

In Jesus' Name, AMEN

The Lord willing, we will go on now to other things.
Hebrews 6:3 LB

Father,

It is a time for growth.

We cannot continue to repeat the basics of the Christian faith over and over again.

We need to inhale the sweet promise of new horizons which will result in greater depth and understanding of the fact that God is here, and involved in our daily battle with life itself.

Father, it is time we stopped repeating doctrine and went on with the vital job of living the Truth which we say we believe.

Help us learn these "other things."

In Jesus' Name, AMEN

And now may the God of peace, who brought again from the dead our Lord Jesus, equip you with all you need for doing his will. May he who became the great Shepherd of the sheep by an everlasting agreement between God and you, signed with his blood, produce in you through the power of Christ all that is pleasing to him. To him be glory forever and ever. Amen.

Hebrews 13:20, 21 LB

Father,

I have heard ministers use this benediction in church, but seeing it in front of my own eyes and trying to grasp the fantastic truth of what You are saying makes me realize how great Your written Word is when it comes *alive* in my heart!

O God, equip me for what I need to do Your will.

May it be Your strength in me which allows me to accomplish that which pleases You.

Even more important, Father, may it be Your strength in me which allows me to *be* that which is pleasing to You.

In Jesus' Name, AMEN

Yes indeed, it is good when you truly obey our Lord's command, "You must love and help your neighbors just as much as you love and take care of yourself."

James 2:8 LB

Father,

It is a clear command of Jesus Christ, and James has reminded me of what Christ said,

        not only to love my neighbor as much as myself—but to help him and take care of him as I would help and take care of myself.

Lord, the comparison is clear. I will try—but I will need Your help!

In Jesus' Name, AMEN

When Jesus came to the place where they were he stopped in the road and called, "What do you want me to do for you?"

"Sir," they said, "we want to see!"

Jesus was moved with pity for them and touched their eyes. And instantly they could see, and followed him.

Matthew 20:32–34 LB

Dear God,

How wonderful that You said to the blind, "What do you want me to do for you?"

So often we ask You to do things for us.

It is beautiful to realize that You were moved by the needs of those who called upon You.

It is reassuring to know that You are moved by the needs of our own hearts as we call upon You.

We, too, want to see.

Thank You for touching us.

In Jesus' Name, AMEN

*We toss the coin, but it is the Lord who controls its
decision.*

Proverbs 16:33 LB

Dear Father,

Sometimes it is difficult to realize that Your overall power
is just that—
overall power!

In Jesus' Name, AMEN

And because of what Christ did, all you others too, who heard the Good News about how to be saved, and trusted Christ, were marked as belonging to Christ by the Holy Spirit, who long ago had been promised to all of us Christians. His presence within us is God's guarantee that he really will give us all that he promised; and the Spirit's seal upon us means that God has already purchased us and that he guarantees to bring us to himself. This is just one more reason for us to praise our glorious God.

Ephesians 1:13, 14 LB

Dear God,

I know that I have been saved by trusting Your Son, Christ.

These verses reaffirm that the Holy Spirit of God actually marked *me* as belonging to You, guaranteed His promises, and put His seal upon me.

It is so easy to think of the Holy Spirit as an influence— but I realize that He is as much God as are the Father and the Son.

Spirit of God, I recognize Your Personhood and thank You.

In Jesus' Name, AMEN

There was a man sent from God, whose name was John.
John 1:6 KJV

Father,

You know my name is not John but I want to be a man
sent from You.

I want to be a man sent from You who can represent You
by word and deed—to put forth the reality of a
living Christ.

Father, help me to be a man who is sent from You.

In Jesus' Name, AMEN

Even so faith, if it hath not works, is dead, being alone.
James 2:17 KJV

Father,

So often I think about and speak about faith.
Lately I have seen people around me who do not make
such a noise about faith.
These people show by their works what they
are.
By their life they trumpet forth the philosophy that grips
their souls.
By their willingness to go further than is expected and by
their concern—
they are saying that they have faith.
I wish to retain my emphasis upon faith, Father. Please
help me to put forth the reality of faith with
works—action!

In Jesus' Name, AMEN

> *The Lord's blessing is our greatest wealth. All our work adds nothing to it!*
>
> Proverbs 10:22 LB

Father,

You have told us to work.

You have told us to work hard, as one who does not need to be ashamed.

As we go about our daily work, Father, help us to remember that—

all we earn in life—

all we hope to have in life—

must be in the perspective that

Your blessing is our greatest wealth.

In Jesus' Name, AMEN

The earth belongs to God! Everything in all the world is his!

Psalms 24:1 LB

Father,

I must apologize for the times I think of You only as a Heavenly being—as the great Creator of the Universe sitting upon a throne in Heaven—looking down upon me on this earth.

I must realize that You live in my heart, and that everything in all the world is Yours.

May I, with proper humility and reverence, live on this planet in such a way that my life will enhance, not degrade it.

In Jesus' Name, AMEN

Righteousness exalteth a nation: but sin is a reproach to any people.

Proverbs 14:34 KJV

Dear God,

I thank You for the privilege I have not only as a citizen of "God's Country," but as a citizen of the United States of America.

I am grateful for the pride I feel when I think of what this Nation has accomplished.

Father, do not let this great Country drift further from the true spiritual moorings which made us what we are.

May I, as a person, and this Nation as a whole, be guided by moral and spiritual objectives. May our righteousness exalt this Nation.

Guide us so that we do not follow the path of expediency and find reproach upon us.

In Jesus' Name, AMEN

Go ahead and prepare for the conflict, but victory comes from God.

Proverbs 21:31 LB

Father,

It is important to be prepared.
You have taught us in the Word of God
      the importance of discipline,
      of being alert,
      and the importance of hearing suggestions
      from counselors.
Yet we realize that when all things are said and done, and
      the conflict is finally over, the victory does indeed
      come from You and You alone.
As we go about our daily tasks help us to remember
      to look to You for the victory.

In Jesus' Name, AMEN

Love does no wrong to anyone. That's why it fully satisfies all of God's requirements. It is the only law you need.

Romans 13:10 LB

Lord,

You tell me that LOVE is "the only law" that I need, and I
   am aware of the importance You place upon this
   word, LOVE, as I read this verse.
God LOVED me first, Christ LOVED me by going to the
   cross, and the Spirit of God LOVES me enough to
   comfort me now.
Help me, Father, to wrap my life up in LOVE that I might
   show forth this LOVE in my life to others.

In Jesus' Name, AMEN

*I would have you learn this great fact: that a life of doing
right is the wisest life there is.*

Proverbs 4:11 LB

Lord,

This verse is unquestionably true.
It is an obvious, overt, clear statement of fact.
    Yet, who can live up to this at all times?
We view this as an awesome responsibility—when we
    should really look at it as an opportunity and a
    privilege.

In Jesus' Name, AMEN

Glory and honor to God forever and ever. He is the King of the ages, the unseen one who never dies; he alone is God, and full of wisdom . . . .

1 Timothy 1:17 LB

Father,

I know that You are full of wisdom and that You are the true God.

You are the true God of Abraham, Isaac, and Jacob,
         the true God of Matthew, Mark, Luke, and John, and *my* God, as well.

May I give You glory and honor not only when it seems appropriate, but when You deserve it—at all times!

In Jesus' Name, AMEN

But God's truth stands firm like a great rock, and nothing can shake it . . . .

2 Timothy 2:19 LB

Dear God,

In this age when men fear bombs that can destroy mountains—accusations that can destroy lives—it is reassuring to know that there is something that cannot be changed:

THE TRUTH OF GOD.

Thank You for showing me the way, the truth, and the life.

In Jesus' Name, AMEN

*Teach us to number our days and recognize how few
they are; help us to spend them as we should.*

Psalms 90:12 LB

Father,

Teach me the value of properly using my time.
In my attempts at enjoying life, may I not waste that of
which I have so precious little—the moments of
each day.

In Jesus' Name, AMEN

Since the Lord is directing our steps, why try to under-
stand everything that happens along the way?

Proverbs 20:24 LB

Lord,

As human beings, we always want to know the *why* of
    everything.

We want to put all the pieces together ourselves, and
    know all the details before they happen—or after
    they have happened—in our lives.

But if we really believe that You are guiding our lives and
    leading us along life's way, we will not always try
    to figure You out.

Forgive me for my human nature that questions. I will do
    my best to question as little as I can.

Help me, Father, to accept Your guiding steps and to walk
    in them.

In Jesus' Name, AMEN

Shout with joy before the Lord, O earth! Obey him gladly; come before him, singing with joy.

Try to realize what this means—the Lord is God! He made us—we are his people, the sheep of his pasture.

Go through his open gates with great thanksgiving; enter his courts with praise. Give thanks to him and bless his name. For the Lord is always good. He is always loving and kind, and his faithfulness goes on and on to each succeeding generation.

Psalms 100:1–5 LB

Dear God,

I am so happy that I can be thankful and grateful to You not only for what You have done for me, but for the kind of God You are.

I thank You that You are not only a mighty, powerful God to be respected and feared by men, but a God in whom we can rejoice, and before whom we come gladly.

I come before You now, Lord, with joyful singing, thanksgiving, and praise!

In Jesus' Name, AMEN

Show respect for everyone. Love Christians every-where. Fear God and honor the government.

1 Peter 2:17 LB

Father,

Teach me to put into practice these action words—
RESPECT
LOVE
FEAR
HONOR.
Lord, in Your way, teach me the priority of the value
concepts behind the phrasing of these words.
O God, may I live this verse in a real way.

In Jesus' Name, AMEN

Shake hands warmly with each other . . . .
Romans 16:16 LB

Lord,

How often do I shake someone's hand without recogniz-
ing him as a person—
a person who needs the warmth of sincerity,
the warmth of concern,
and the warmth of knowing that he is important to me.
Since this is Your command, Lord, I fully comprehend
that this person is important to You or You would
never have encouraged me to shake his hand
warmly—You would never have shown Your great
love by the act of joining our hands with Yours
through the nail-pierced hands of Your Son.

In Jesus' Name, AMEN

You can never please God without faith, without de-pending on him. Anyone who wants to come to God must believe that there is a God and that he rewards those who sincerely look for him.

Hebrews 11:6 LB

Dear God,

You know that I wish to have faith. But I am constantly challenged because so much that I face on this earth demands that I accept things based upon certain acts of reason.

Father, in spite of all the logical proofs and discussions about Your existence, I realize that I still must take that final step of "saving" faith.

Help me, Father, to take that step, and teach me to have faith and daily dependence on You.

In Jesus' Name, AMEN

*Now you are no longer strangers to God and foreigners
to heaven, but you are members of God's very own family,
citizens of God's country, and you belong to God's household with every other Christian.*

Ephesians 2:19 LB

Dear God,

I am especially appreciative of the fact that I am a citizen
of Your Country.

I realize my heritage as an American and that I am a citizen of this country because I was born here.

I am also a citizen of Your Country, Lord, because I was
born into Your Family by the act of faith and
through receiving Jesus Christ.

I am grateful that I am not a foreigner to You.

Help me to be a better citizen, both here in America, and
in Your Country.

In Jesus' Name, AMEN

He was before all else began and it is his power that holds everything together.

Colossians 1:17 LB

Father,

When I think of the omnipotence of Your Son, Jesus Christ, I think of it as a doctrine and a theological idea that may sometimes be difficult to understand.

But Father, when You say the power of Christ holds everything together, it must also mean *me* as well.

Your omnipotent power holds not only the vastness of the universe and the many worlds flung into space—*it holds me.*

Just me—and those around me—and those around the world.

You are a God who is big enough to hold the universe together, and still concerned enough to hold *me* together.

Thank You, dear Lord.

In Jesus' Name, AMEN

Open my eyes to see wonderful things in your Word.
Psalms 119:18 LB

Father,

Your Word is there day after day—
        sitting upon a shelf,
        gathering dust upon a table,
        lying in that desk drawer.
Teach me to open my eyes that I might see those wonderful things Your Word has to offer me, Lord.
Open my eyes, I pray, to things I have read time and again, but have never really seen.

In Jesus' Name, AMEN

Your steadfast love, O Lord, is as great as all the heavens. Your faithfulness reaches beyond the clouds.

Psalms 36:5 LB

Dear Lord,

The heavens I can see.

The clouds I can see.

But to comprehend, Lord, that Your love is *that* large, and Your faithfulness goes further than the clouds above—as I look up even now, it amazes me!

Your Word tells us in another place, "great is Thy faithfulness."

It certainly must be, to be *that* extending.

Thank You for Your steadfast and great love, and for proving Your limitless faithfulness.

In Jesus' Name, AMEN

But those who do what Christ tells them to will learn to love God more and more. That is the way to know whether or not you are a Christian. Anyone who says he is a Christian should live as Christ did.

1 John 2:5, 6 LB

Father,

The standard You set for me is impossible—
>I cannot live as Your Son did, for He was perfect.

Yet, I know that even Christ was tempted.
>May He be my goal—
>May He be my aim—
>May I strive to live as He lived, and each day, learn to love You, my God, more and more.

In Jesus' Name, AMEN

The wicked will finally lose; the righteous will finally win.

Proverbs 21:18 LB

Lord,

It is sometimes difficult, as I look around, to understand this verse.

I suppose this is because I have spiritual tunnel vision. I cannot see very far ahead.

Because You are God, You are not bothered by the twenty-twenty vision of human nature.

You have the ability to see beyond the close of nightfall, beyond the New Year's Eves of tomorrow and say, "The righteous will finally win." And, Lord, *I do believe it!*

In Jesus' Name, AMEN

You know how full of love and kindness our Lord Jesus was: though he was so very rich, yet to help you he became so very poor, so that by being poor he could make you rich.

2 Corinthians 8:9 LB

Lord,

Your Son is the only one I know who would go riches to
rags so that I might go rags to riches.
Because Your Son humbled Himself and became a man,
died the embarrassing death on the cross,
and rose again from the dead—
I am, through faith, allowed to become His child.
Father, Your Son was full of love and kindness.
Teach me the importance and the truth of allowing this
love and kindness to radiate to others, with whom I
come in contact in my daily life.

In Jesus' Name, AMEN

Lord! Help! Godly men are fast disappearing. Where in all the world can dependable men be found?

Psalms 12:1 LB

Father,

The cry of David is Your cry today.

In an age when people *expect* to be disappointed by insincerity in others, we are asked, "Where can dependable men be found?"

Lord, the answer, I believe, is in men of Yours. Men who depend upon You for their sustenance, their strength, and their power.

Be these things to me, Lord.

Help me be the kind of man who will ruin the averages about Your kind of godly men disappearing.

Thank You for being concerned about me enough to want me to be a man of Yours.

Guide me, I pray.

In Jesus' Name, AMEN

*You were getting along so well. Who has interfered with
you to hold you back from following the truth? It certainly
isn't God who has done it, for he is the one who has called
you to freedom in Christ.*

Galatians 5:7, 8 LB

O Lord,

Isn't it interesting how sometimes I look to You as the
source of my blessing?

And at other times I look to You as someone who is interfering in such a way that it causes me problems?

I realize that this attitude toward You is unfair.

You have said in Your Word that You might chastise or
purge men for their own good.

Each individual allows different things to interfere with
his following the truth.

Father, I pray that with Your help the goal of freedom in
Christ is a reachable goal.

Supply me with strength so that I will not excuse myself because something is interfering
with my progress.

In Jesus' Name, AMEN

May my spoken words and unspoken thoughts be pleas-
ing even to you, O Lord my Rock and my Redeemer.
Psalms 19:14 LB

Lord,

My spoken words are more likely to be pleasing to You
    and to others, than my unspoken thoughts.
Pleasing unspoken thoughts—now that's a different story.
Unspoken thoughts are often just that—thought I do not
    want to put into words.
Often I feel a man can read unspoken thoughts, and You
    always can de-motivate them.
Father, make both my spoken words and my unspoken
    thoughts pleasing to You.

In Jesus' Name, AMEN

INDEX